Life, Romance & Poetry

Chris A. Misdary

Baltimore, Maryland

Life, Romance & Poetry

Copyright © 1995 Chris A. Misdary

All rights reserved under International and Pan-American copyright conventions. No part of this book may be reproduced, stored in a retrieval system, or transmitted in any form, electronic, mechanical, or other means, now known or hereafter invented, without written permission of the author. Address all inquiries to the publisher.

Library of Congress
Cataloging in Publication Data
ISBN 1-56167-201-7
Library of Congress Card Catalog Number:
95-068003

Published by

8019 Belair Road, Suite 10
Baltimore, Maryland

Manufactured in the United States of America

Table of Contents

Foreword ix

Classic Romance 1
Windy Eve 3
Mystery of Romance 4
Times of the Valley 6
Three Magics 7
Glamour 7
Revealing Who's She 8
The Crying Mississippi 9
Oh, Mother 10
Self Conviction 12
Picture of Tears 12
Sough of Memory 13
Nature & Beauty 15
Memory Recall 15
Wedding at Eclipse 16
Who's I Who's She 17
Nights of Memory 18
Cyclamen 18
Dove 19
Commitment 19
A Soft Wave 20
Road to Paradise 21
Free-dome 22
Heart & Tears 23
Doubt & Answer 24
Fashion 25

Archeology, Society Politics, and History 27
Lotus 29
Soul of Courage 29
Head High 30
Lesson of History 31
Voice of Ancient 31

Wake Up Call 32
Voice of the Homeless 33
Satan of Koresh 34
We the People We the Guard 35
Mathematical-Constitution 36
Thomas Jefferson's 250th Birthday 37
Ben is Here 38
In the Mind of "Abe's" 39
J.F.K. 40
Jaqueline & Dream 41
F.D.R. 42
Immigrant 43
At Last 43
Deed of Demand 44
Hope 44
Song of Martin 45
Vote! 45
Voyager 46
To Saddam with Love 47
Vote & Deed 47
Fission 48
Infants 48
Words of Truth 49
The 1992 Presidential Campaign 51
Comeback-Kid, Combat-Kid, & Mr. Kid 53
Inauguration Song 54
104 Congress and Majority 55
Three Rivers 57
North Star 57
Sphinx 58
Cosmos, Age, & Observations 59
Witness of Society 60

Light Romance   61
Dance & Romance 63
Paradise 64
Place in the Heart 65
Oh Lady 66

Summer of Love 67
Romance 67
No More 68
In the Wind 69
A Desire 70
Why? 71
Heavenly Eyes 71
Want You 72
Such You 73
Silent Night 73
Won't Ask Why? 74
You Are 74
Bartender 75
Promises 76
Life Ordeal 77
Adam and Eve 78
How Could I? 78
Lifetime 79
Love Song 79
Up Side-Down 80

Philosophy & Thoughts   81
The Three Elements 83
Evolution, Revolution Into Re- 84
Universe, Sea, and Stone 84
Fate 85
Life & Thoughts 86
Wise Man 86
Such Man's! 87
Logic 87
Man and Free 88
Life 88
Reasoning 89
Birthday 89
Man! 90
Dust & Earth 90
Wine & Wheat 91
Power of Thee Word 92

Words of Wisdom 93
Baseball 94

Children & Religion 97
The Joys of the Seasons 99
One Two Three 100
Learning 101
The High-Rank 102
The Kids 102
Prayers & Wonders 103
Mary & Son 104
Again We'll Meet 105
Over Come the Death ("The Christ") 104

The Four Seasons 107
Winter 109
Spring 109
Summer 110
Autumn 110

Afterward 111

Foreword

First let me thank you for your curiosity and for buying my book; and by the way, it is yours now, so take a look. I hope you enjoy it and keep it close at hand.

Second, please and with all welcome let us travel on a journey of thoughts, into the roads of human lives and purpose, so into the beyond.

As a poet I am very honored to share with you my poetry, which is often based on reality, often on what is personal and private.

Third and before I tell you about myself as a poet, please let me express what I believe about poetry. **Poetry** and **time** are powerful tools of simple knowledge taken from history. Through them we see evidence and finger prints from the time of King David to the Sophists to the time of Socrates, and into modern history from Shakespeare until now. Poetry is always the art of society expressed through music and song, and poetry has always had its own part in forming our Democratic World. It has always spoken out against tyrannies and oppressive rule or rulers. Above all, **a true poet** has the **Gift of God of Mind**, so it is with **truth** that the true poet always aims high with **society** in the time of prosperity.

Now it is time for me to tell you who I am as your poet and in what I believe. I was born in Egypt of Coptic Orthodox parentage, which is also the Christian faith in its oldest of forms. My parents were a great influence on me, but as a poet and student of philosophy I have always focused my thoughts on the God that is found in the truth and means of the Christian faith.

I truly believe that the Christian faith is comparable with every element of human life and with every stage of life, and, I might add, Christianity is the soul basis of what the Jews believe and the beliefs of the ancient Egyptians. It is not difficult to see the connection.

When I came to America on March 10, 1980 my poetry was only in my mind and in my heart. When I began experimenting with the American culture I promised myself I would look at the culture through both the eyes of a child and the eyes of an adult. I consider the date of my arrival in America to be my second birth, which was by my **choice**.

Leading to my book of poetry, which was inspired by Ancient Egypt and Christian morals, I must admit that I was also inspired by the great American Constitution. I have found it to be along the same line and concept as my morals and values. I hope that the following examples will demonstrate these concepts and will, perhaps, allow us a clear view of them.

American Constitution
It is the power of the **Triangle** or **Three Dimensions** as a divine power of:
1. Executive   2. Legislative   3. Judicial

All of these are under the power of the consent of the **Fourth Dimension**—"We the People."
No Vote=No Democracy.

Christian Beliefs
It is the power of the **Triangle** or **Three Dimensions** as a divine power of:
1. God   2. Holy Spirit   3. Christ

All three are **Equals** which also share the existence of power of the **Fourth Dimension** which is Mary, the Mother.
No Mary=None.

Ancient Pyramids
Are the power of **Four Dimensions** or **Four Triangles**. Into a **Circle** "360-Degrees" we can only see **three dimensions**, or one **triangle** therefore being altered. Again this is representative of the power of the **Fourth Element** and **Beyond.**
No Fourth Dimension=No Pyramid

Nature
Is a **Fourth Dimension** of:
1. Water   2. Earth   3. Air

And all through the **Power** of the **Fourth Element** or **Dimension** there is **Fire**.
No Fire=No Creation.

There are too many examples and facts based on this same idea, which I hope you will find throughout my poetry. God willing, there will be more examples and details about this in my next book.

Now, my friend and reader, I feel that you should know about my own beliefs and the moral reasonings which have influenced my thoughts and ignited my liberty.

I believe that:

> The voice of the people . . .
> is the God voice.
>
> Through, Man's rising or falling . . .
> Is the man and matter of choice.

The next example is one I learned from my parents.

> "Do not dig down and under corner stones, nor throw sand into wind; both fall down over head or into eyes!"

My parents also taught me about **life** as such:

> "Man's life is Man's gift . . .
> In such a Sun;
> and Sun rise, for never sit!"

* * *

In the end and above all I do believe that **"God is Love"** and love is the basic element of humanity. By the way, **"We are all human"** even with different beliefs.

I hope you enjoy this **journey. Thanks.**

Poet Chris A. Misdary

Classic Romance

Windy Eve

Once at windy eve...
      So fearful was its sound

Carrying my load on lonely road...
      Overcast with emptiness in the background

Walking the sun to its set...
      Overleaping oneself into cloudy bound

Walking the sun to its set...
      Once upon a time in mind

Looking through welkin far behind...
      To rubble of life left me astound

Follow the mirage fading away...
      Thou running after and falling behind

Holding the dark with no sense for touch...
      Even it's shaping the silence all around

Seeking the love with bleeding heart...
      Flooding eyes with tears and drowned

Through life memorabilia into past...
      Conjure the conscience & in soul remain insight profound

Mystery of Romance

Into the mystery between rays and shadow...
    Full moon was glowing through my dormer window

Evenfall shading the blue curtain, after sundown...
    Alluring romance of bosomy hills, blustered her gown

Heavenly face with a peaceful smile...
    With sweet odors, such incense of the Nile

The gypsy-hair, as a soft air touching free...
    Free waves take me into the depth of sea

Eyes to eyes, bluish lips, and the taste of wine...
    Hands to hands, whispering voices, and no con fine!!!

TWIN BUT ONE: MARRIAGE VOW

When my morning is coming through...
    The first thing I want see, is You...

When The Sun, reaching The Heart, Into The Blue...
    I want nothing else...but You

So, When The Star, from far, such candle of the night...
    And you between my arms...so my sight

Through Full Moon, And shining on the Sea...
    I want all of You...to have all of me

Thou, we breaks, the Handcuffs, and be what's be...
    So, we sense every touch, Such a Twin, But One... and free.

DREAMS

We were going...uptown
Climbing the hills...
    And running down

We were kissing...and clown
So we swim...
    In River of love...and drown

I still go to...the same place
With hope of heart...or just in case
    At any case...I see your face.

So, with sense of touch...
dreams or much...
Such, flying birds in blue space.

BETWEEN BOTH!

Blue eyes, such seas...
    High waves, and spicy taste

Brown eyes, such Rivers...
    Waveless & deep, thou refreshing mist

Blue eyes, such weather & skies...
    Every lover's eager to know

Brown eyes, such earth & real...
    Real to touch, and much so.

Between both, never such, overdose...
    More & more, I come close,
    More & less, I have my cause.

Times of the Valley

Watched the sun at early rising...
      Rising through its welkin & into the sky
Sending warmth to the valley & shining...
      With golden rays on the road, for you & I

The birds flying, so landing...
      For morning dance, over the trees
With musical sounds, they were singing...
      The song of love, for morning ease

Slowly the cloud was moving...
      Moving the shade & passing through
With light rain & sprinkling...
      Thou the light wind comes and flew

The breezy air was soft and blowing...
      Touching the hair, as softness as be
Through *evenshade into welkin...
      Watched the sun, fading away & free
But free was of my thinking...
      That tomorrow's coming suns...
      Will come again of the far sea.

*Evenshade = twilight

Three Magics

Love, self, and desire...
    Are three motions in-one-element...
    And each is such a frame of require

Sometimes they're such heaven-on-earth...
    and in others, they're such a burning fire

Meanwhile, for honoring their magical elements...
    Much faith for the holiness is eminent to inspire

Although, as term for analogy perhaps...
    For one-short-element of those will go hand in hand...
    For such is the emperor without his empire!!!

Glamour

As the beauty of the roses...
sometime, will expire

As well the green leaves...
will go dry, sear, and drier

But forever, the romance of your eyes...
stays in the heart, like a flaming fire.

Revealing Who's She

Revealing to reverie, who is she,
Looking far to her red golden hair,
In the wind flaring and waving free,
She's the sun in romantic kiss,
Between the arms of the sea!

Revealing to reverie, who is she,
Standing nude in the valley,
With candling sky, so moon can see,
Perhaps the fall knows that her nudity,
Will enforce the winter, for the long nights,
For her beauty kneeling down on the knee!

Revealing to reverie, who is she,
moving clouds shading the curtains,
For the early shower, for she!

Revealing to reverie, who is she,
Wearing a new gown, waiting her Valentine,
Coming down, from far away of the Apogee,
Holding the flowers of the Spring,
For rendezvous, with she the 'sweet-odor' the tree!

Revealing to reverie, who is she,
Looking to the sun of Summer,
Expanding her wings, to shade her lover,
To cool of the heat, and flee!
To the children she says, come and play,
And if you get tired, on my lap stay,
Or take a nap, and let your head lean on me,
I welcome all, young and old, even the stinging bee!

Revealing to reverie, who's she,
The only one Mother, was born from ever,
And for ever, she will be,
Her love and anger, must remember, from 'A' to 'Z',
She's the 'nature', she's 'us', she's 'we'!

The Crying Mississippi

Was a late of the day, and early in summer...
Through the stormy wind, I was hearing the sound...
Emerging from drowning farms and falling ground...
Falling down into the Mississippi River.

I said to him...Why this anger...or the rally...
And why with your tears you romancing the valley.
Does you breaking the silence for cheers...
Or you breaking out of your fears.

But the time has gone by...
And the mighty river not answering the why...
Even though, with try after try...
The burst thunder...such fire in the heart of the sky.
And once a while...
Through this trial.
So unmerciful the rain was coming down...
And the poor river, with both arms...holding every town
Seemingly, such a king losing his crown...
Or such a queen, with shredded gown.

So again...and again
With round after round of the rain...
The crying Mississippi such giant taken the pain...
And looking to me, with feeling that in vain.
I said sorry oh mighty...
It's not you...
But us that we lives insane!

Oh, Mother
PART I

To whom...am I...
Would laugh, or cry
Evermore thorn, for the try.

Fearing to reason, so the why
Defusing the secrecy, for comply
The burning desire, of last bye-bye

But the core of the matter...
No one, for what so ever
Accept & receiving me...just you oh, Mother.

Now the fact...You're gone away
And endless became my sorrow
Thou, soundless of my say!

Through, mist of my dejection...
I'm hearing a pray
With sparkling smile...
Such spectrum...such full moon sending the ray
Endued my broken heart, with soul speaking not to fey

In me felt your bless...
Candling the dark of the nights
And shining the sun of my days
Lighting tomorrow, thus, leading the way.

* In honor of my mother's death, so my soul mentor. God bless her and all who are there.

Flaming Candle in the Heart
PART II:

No...for saying never
No...for the no more & never
No...for these burning words, thou foolish endeavor.

But, yes memory, and fact of matter
Flaming candle in the heart, for you oh. Mother

Oh. Mother, looking then to all those years
Your shining smile, seemingly as now in appears
Lighten tomorrow with hope, taking away my fears
Oh. Mother, such rose of beauty...such love forever near.

Self Conviction

Alongshore of my thought...
A question with my predication!

Does the fear of tomorrow...
Fearfully, comes out of the rejection!

Or that the heart being self prisoner...
Thus, a hostage to his own fiction!

Does the past form away shading the shadow...
And reviving today with own nail of crucifixion!

Or the soul through the pain of love...
Though, sensing the depth of guilt, so self conviction!

Picture of Tears

Why won't listen to the heart of mine...
    And why won't shed tears, even I'm crying
Thou, all that happen...
    Into the order of time
Thou, all that begin...
    Since I wrote you, my own rhyme.

I see no tears...
    But shadow in my eye
Making picture of your appears...
    And through the eye drops of my.

Sough of Memory

Same time in this day...
For some years ago

Remembered the moon was shining...
So the reflection of your eyes

When you told me...
Hold me, and don't ask why too

Thou, while my hands holding you...
And my eyes looking at you...
I wished to say...I love you!

Same time in this day...
For a few years ago

We were walking...
Whispering through talking

When you told me...
Hold me, and never let me go

Thou, while my hands holding you...
And my eyes looking at you...
I have said...I love you!!

Same time in this day...
Not for long ago

Your head was on my shoulder...
So, my arms rounding you tight & stronger

When you told me...
For last kiss me, I'm now with you

Thou, while my hands holding you...
And my eyes looking at you...
I said...I have always loved you!!!

Nature & Beauty

The nature is gifted you the beauty,
From her own, so with render.

Life in your eyes, reflecting into stormy hills,
With arcing bolts, lightening and thunder.

Living Rose, taste out of your lips,
Such the wants, growing wild, thou wieldier.

Since the day, we have met,
My heart has gone, to the land of wander.

I feel baseless, to let the time bypass,
Nor is wise, for the time, I surrender.

For such life...such time...such days,
Is such tomorrow...is such now,
Thou, the past...is such from above to under!

Memory Recall

The count is down,
For the New Year
And with every going second
To the last-one will appear
The feeling is over casting my fear
For spurring heart, and pulsing with a spear.

With depth inside me, so my soul
A touch of memory for recall
That's my love, such the rose in the Spring
But yours, just a searing leaf in the Fall!

Wedding at Eclipse

The shining moon in blue sky
His wishes to romance earth
But, earth for his romance, remains shy

At the time and the place
She's covering her face
With veil made out of space

Waiting for the king
To bring her the ring
With chaplain sing

Her wedding is a dream
In chapel full of gleam

With chaplet of every star
Holding the candles of the solar

The bride is full of desire
And the groom heart's sitting on fire

Since the zero time of the expand
And the signature of the deed at demand
That again they will touch in holding hand

Since the time of the separation
After the fact of the creation
Was a promise of marriage & integration
In ceremony at eclipse, for the reincarnation

Who's I
Who's She

The revealing to reverie,
Who? is she.
Such a fading cloud,
And shadow of tree.

Revealing to reverie,
That the crying eyes,

Was full of tears,
And eye drops, with humble-bee.

* * *

Such rains, into ocean,
Such silent of devotion
Such waves in stormy sea.

* * *

The revealing to reverie,
Who's am I,

I am a free spirit,
With apposition to blue sky

I'm a bird, into the fly,
Thou, the broken wing,

And the gusty wind,
Will strengthen, my fly.

Nights of Memory

I fear the night, so my heart...
    I fear too many things, since we became apart

Every time I go to my bed...
    I remember every word,
    At once we have said

Why...through the tears of my eyes...
    I drew your picture of my cries

I want to run away, but where I go...
    You are everywhere with me,
    Such my ghost...Such my shadow...And such so.

Cyclamen

I walked into her room...
Cyclamen in everywhere, with full bloom

Hearing music, and softly sound...
Shakes my steps, thou moves my ground

Walked to her, with my all desire...
Thirsty for love, such heart in flaming fire

Into passage door, to the temple of her throne...
Candle lights, Crystal window, and both we alone.

Dove

O, mon amour...O, my love
O, sweetheart...I'm your Dove

Every kiss...I wish not to miss
More or less...Are yours

Every touch...And every such
More and much...All for you

O, mon amour...O, mon amie
I'm hoping 'n' love...You & me.

Commitment

Into the nights; And memory's in the heart...
    Even with love & its shadow; So A Bleeding-Dart

Fearing the silence of the time, So the Route...
    With firing causes between my ribs, So my sight,
    So fueling me, To shout & shout

Sensing the time of tomorrow, With no doubt...
    Thou, A Witness of its value; And for no time to
    runs out

But with no fears of the distance; Nor we apart...
    Thus, the journey is the same,
    And the destiny is just equals; And so we start.

A Soft Wave

Whom to you am I...
It's an eve thought, even with no why!

No why; no reason to explain...
For fearing of reverse...
Or losing the happy pain!

Whom to me you are...
It feels like the sound of touch...
Coming closer from away & far!

Away & far, but lives at heart...
Such the twin at the mind...
Even if we are kept apart!

You to me...
Such the dawn of day...
Such a spiritual sight.

Road to Paradise

Between the arms of the valley...
    And a random of light, holding a silent tree
It takes away the fear of my rally...
    For shying looks into balmy tree, breezing and free
The playful wing shaking the hair...
    Though with majesty of touch & sound of blare
And from above and far...
    The spirit of guard & the North Star
Holding the shining sword...
    Standing tall and bold
Swearing and more...
    Aiming high on her shore
Though, anyone must be fit...
    Before entering to her door
Thou, the door is the step to paradise...
    Into heavenly road, such sun shines into crystal ice.

*To the tune of **Lady Liberty**.

Free-dome
PART I

Reading the word "freedom"...
    but in my heart's a "free-dome."
Though, "dome" is the expression of the sky...
    and "free" is the home.

Some call it freedom...
    and I call it free-dome
It's my constitutional right...
    & my right is fact, though, not assume.

*To the tune of the *Bill of Rights*.

Free-dome's Soul
PART II

What's a democracy, with no freedom of speech...
    & what's truth, if truth no to be leash.
What's an art, if there's no art of word...
    & what's freedom, into a silence of death and cold.
Ever have we imagined...
    if we lived without our Constitution-wagon.
Though, does America will be as of now...
    or will be as the same time of the dragon.
Thinking of the Bill of Rights...
    & its power force of the might.
Thinking again, but sure so quite...
    this is the freedom-soul,
    and shines in such candlelight.

Heart & Tears

I have waited for you...
    Until the time became in such heavy feet.

I waited for you...
    And with hope of heart, you and I will meet.

Thinking of the past, and with desire of the at last...
At last and not a fake, nor shall be rebate
    And into Ocean of my romance
    The heart was sailing and free
    Free and moving into dance
    In such wind, touching branches of tree.

I waited for you...
And in such a bird, I was flying into eve.
Into eve, into nest of my silence...
In such cold, and mist of grief
    And into River of my romance
    I was sailing into fears
    Fearing the soul and its enhance
    Enhancing the heart and into tears.

I waited for you...
    Until the shadow runaway from me
So, in such face passing through...
    A cloudy shape, I can't touch, I can't see.

Doubt & Answer

What a meaning of the spring...
    If the birds can't fly & sing.
What a flower ! If flowers can't grow...
    & what a poem! If the poem with no prose.

What a life! If life is not within...
    & what a sea! If there's no waves & motion therein.

What a destiny! If no road to begin...
    & what a lion! If the lion have no den.

What a love! If not to share so free...
    & what the "I"! If "I" alone without "we."

What a tomorrow! If today is not to be...
    & what the past! If past has lost its key.

And why the doubt! If that the answer...
    In such math, having the "One"
    And adding the "Two" make them Three!

Fashion

The party is not over...
    Nor am I a feather in the wind
And so if I have bent over...
    Never I thought, will come to end!
Though, the only reason for maneuver...
    Was only for the sake of my friend
Friend, and into same endeavor...
    Have the say, and sharing the recommend.
So perhaps, if I sought to win you over...
    It's moreover, it is the fashion to defend!

Archeology, Society Politics, and History

Lotus

Always in my heart, so my depth,
"DALLAS" is such a Flour of "LOTUS,"
And its "Book Depository" is a hand of DEATH.

There, was a great Man,
His time has set, at his dawn; Though Rebirth.

Through, a Flaming Torch, and Soul of wealth,
The magic of his own, so his myth,
Such a story, holding the time, with great length.

Soul of Courage

Such Love and Heart of kindness...
    Need no sorrow, even thou the sadness

Person to Person, I wasn't fortunate to know...
    But no doubt, She's a Soul of courage & much so

Thus, the only thing I have regret...
    That we ever have met, yet.

So, to the Soul of you "Virginia"...
    I wish to say how I felt

Feeling you, is the same of my own...
    warmth, Inspiration, and love fully reflect

Reflecting in heart, So the mind...
    Such the rising Sun, even at the set.

Head High

Head high...
With soar spirit and fly

Head high...
With solid feet on my track...

Counting every step...
Even thou, heavy cross on my back

Head high...
And tomorrow under my eye...
Looking to then...
For some to learn...
And have the now not to go by

Head high...
With strong wings...
Not afraid to fall...
Even thou the fall...
Strengthening again & again to try
Head high...head high...head high

Lesson of History

That the lesson of history,
Has a merit and indication

To the beaten drums of time,
So with the calculation

That constituted arts & politics
As thermometers of definition

For reading the rising & falling,
To every empire, so every nation.

Voice of Ancient

Century twenty one is soon coming to play...
Thus, for women is the Cleopatra lighting ray

Through history of mankind, the man of gender...
Enforces his logic hood of denaturalize to conquer

Making the god of his image, what I wonder...
Thou, that reality has gone to the land of wander

Christian believe 'God was a word' some for reminder...
And the fact of 'a word' is have no race, nor gender

Simple fact is no existence without sister...
Christ's son of mother, thus we're before & after

Wake Up Call

CONGRESS DANCE

Mad ghosts...
Having the roast
Playing with fire...
For self desire

Toasting the wine...
Want us to believe, they crying
With loud voices...
Taking advantage at our crisis

Dancing the evil dance...
Seems a way of their romance
The alligator tears...
In their eyes, only appears

Scares us from the thugs...
Only, to hide the problems under the rugs
Bosnia, Haiti, and Somalia...
Only, are their paraphernalia

Wake America and we the people...
Our congress, a story of 'Cain & Able'
Wake up America, wake up my people...
Wake to the call...before all be disable

Voice of the Homeless

I have a house, but have no home...
I have a room, buy my roof's sky dome!

My bed's a cardboard...
Old & rotten, so full of mold.
It is my shade in summer...
It is my cover in the cold.
It is my companion into the nights...
And it is my pillow, thou my household!

I have no house, I have no land...
I need a job, not hand-outs-hand.
I live in free land...
And what's freedom mean, with no stand.
So to all of you, my fellow American, and my grands...
Some of us poor and have no right,
And though, we have no demand!!!

Satan of Koresh

This is a poetic word,
Has inspired by the Lord!

That the angel of death,
Has got his wish,
Through the Satan of Koresh!

So the angel of life,
By the power of the triumph,
Displayed mercy to Satan,
But Satan in his sane was handcuffed!

What is amuse, and out of excuse,
That the game of blame,
Has begun with the flame,
Singing the song, with devil tongue,
Playing the blues!

Even though, the town of Waco,
And the followers of loco (Wacko)
Burning the fire, such time of 'Hulagu'!

(Hulagu is the grandson of Genghis Khan, also the emperor who in the year 1258, destroyed Baghdad.)

* To the tune of **Waco, Texas Cults**.

We the People
We the Guard

Oh America...and united we stand
Oh mother liberty...on free land.

Of one banner
We the people
We the nation
We the guard.

Our skies and seas...our river and tree
Forever are free...forever we demand.

Of one banner
We the people
We the nation
We the guard.

With devotion...for now and tomorrow
Young and old...all hand in hand.

Of one banner
We the people
We the nation
We the guard.

*To the tune of the National Anthem, "The Star Spangled Banner"

Mathematical-Constitution

Our Constitution; and in such math...
    Framed at perfect, to truth the false & clear the path
Twenty-seven amendments are framed, so ought to be...
    For its purity of actions, is the man & the free.

Looking to its equations...
    Into its numbers of participations
Easy, the facts will be found & agree...
    With each stage & element, is meant us, and we.

The Bill of Rights in ten (10)...
    Zero is the base; one is the value,
Though, base & value, are fact & ten (10).

Added the rest, so total the twenty-seven...
    They come with all facts, and for reason were given.
Three times three times three...
Equal to twenty-seven with law
Three power of two + three power of two + the same one more...
Equal to twenty-seven, so the concept of core
Three in the power of three...
Also equals to twenty-seven, so the sign of you & me.

This is a fact of math, so the mythology of the same...
    Though, it is "us," and "us" must not be "political game"!

$$* * *$$

$3 \times 3 \times 3 = 27$
$3^2 + 3^2 + 3^2 = 27$
$3^3 = 27$

Thomas Jefferson's 250th Birthday

As today is now, and was tomorrow...
As it's then, and called time of zero

From zero to zero is endless end...
So, from zero to unlimited...
Goes the numbers and follow

At base of formative element...
But life & time are named birth...
Into formation to modifying element named death

Three elements are informs circle of time...
While time is exist at begin to begin...
Even though with reversible data...
That time itself can not be reverse!!!

(This poem is a dedication to his soul, which lives with us in a visible sound through his visionary thoughts and living words.)

Ben is Here

Once upon a time...
And into a dream, I visited "Ben"
Though, in such majesty of inter act...
"Ben" is a lightened soul, true, and fact.

The depth of his voice...
Left me with no choice
No choice to sleep into the raft...
No choice, but to defend his craft.

Once upon a time...
And into such a dream, I visited "Ben"
In such reality of light & gleam...
"Ben" is there; "Ben" is here & within.

He asks for the time of now...
With bitterness, asked my why and how
Why we became in such empty den...
And why we turning the time back to then.

"Ben" is here, into his art of word...
Lives into constitution in such sound of gold.
"Ben" is here & on his soul I have my vow...
Vow's standing to his vision, and doesn't matter how!!!

* "Ben" is Benjamin Franklin

In the Mind of "Abe's"

OBSTRUCTIONISTS ARE!

Obstructionists; And "Lincoln" will say...
You're not my team, nor it wasn't my play

"Abe"; And spirit of soul, So life & well...
Asking for looking tomorrow, or the past will

Obstructionists; And obstructionism belief...
Empty substance, and no goals to achieve

Obstructionist; And the arts of the game...
Just shouting-up, with self-pity claim

Obstructionists; And pointing-fingers, taste Myrrh....
Derails the issues, with side blocks to stir

Obstructionist; And look at the speck of sawdust...
When all the time, planks in own eye, thou distrust

Obstructionists; And pharisaical tone...
Such falling leafs, into wind, failing alone

J.F.K.

I did not die...
So, I'm asking not to cry

Won't tears, nor weeps on my grave...
I'm soul and a life...
At my circle I'm a brave

I'm this wind at soft breeze...
With the lighten sun at morning ease
I'm a shines moon at nights...
Such silver lights at waves of seas

I', the gentle rains at Autumn's...
And a glittered diamond at Winter's snows
I'm the free bird at the fly...
So, the star at the beyond of reaching high

No I did not die...
And you won't cry...
Thou, through you I'm here...
Here, such grain at ripened...
Such all of you I'm such I & I.

(God bless his soul.)

Jaqueline & Dream

For you, I wish to light my candle...
For you, I wish to plant the rose

For such you, is such the soft of angel...
Such Jackie, such a dream, and such cause.

The living echoes out of the past...
Coming with every sound, so at last.

From seas into valleys, so every sight...
The smile of you, Oh Jackie, lives in the heart.

Such romance of sweet river, such tree in the height...
Such poetic song of silver moon & golden light.

JACQUELINE & HISTORY, you're pages of bright...
Thou, the nation peace at time the nation was twilight.

(This poem was inspired by and dedicated to the former First Lady, Mrs. Jacqueline B. Kennedy-Onassis. Indeed she has lifted a nation from the darkness of its own sin...This is a deed. May God bless her soul with glory!)

F.D.R.

Does fifty years of history, is that far...
      And perhaps if it's not,
      It is the vision of F. D. R.
It is a revolution and fact...
      With no illusions in contrast
It is the people, with no fear of the fear...
      Thus the F. D. R.'s living words will never sear!
It is "For the People," and they are...
      Are free in the land of liberty & the north star.
Thus, by "the people" & of "the people" was the F. D. R.
      Though, it is a legacy of Democracy and by far!!!

* This poem is dedicated to his soul on his fiftieth anniversary.

Immigrant

Says; Comes, if you're free, or you're poor...
Said; Go Ahead, and reach their free shore.

Says; Comes, leave the desert & hot sand...
    Leave the mirage & handcuff on your hand
Said; Go my son of ancient
    Go, she said, "Go & the shining ray of your way"
    Holding the candle & for you she's stand.

Says; Come & into the art of words, you'll have say...
Said; And if it is so, the truth is the art of the play.
Says; Comes, we have the opening arms, night & day...
Said; Go, I gave you love out of the Nile...
    And go she said, "Hold the Mississippi & Amazon"
    And you will not be alone to display,
    Go...she said "You have my pray."

At Last

"THAT TORCH HAS PAST..."
    Thou, Tomorrow has begun at last
These thee words, such sound into light...
    Thou, Inspiration of the "J.&R.F.K'S" into sight

From the North Castle on the Ice...
    To the South Palaces of Paradise
Into the West, and Golden Sea...
    From the East so the Rising Sun & Free.

"THAT TORCH HAS PAST..."
Is a lasting novel, for tomorrow it has cast.

Deed of Demand

To government "of the people"...
With my freedom of expression...
And with liberty of stand.

And "by the people"...
Is the basis of my case...
The life source of free land.

So that "for the people"...
Is the fact and deed...
And its poem the core of demand.

These are the three democratic elements...
Thus, Jefferson's legacy and with fate of God!

Hope

Hope, is not only a word,
But attitude, for man to cope.

Hope, is a dream of the pharaoh,
So, the Pyramid and triangles of hope.
Hope, was Moses's freedom core,
To free his people, out the Red Sea slope.

Hope, is The Sun of Mary,
And The Messiah over the globe.

Hope, is a little town in Arkansas,
Fueling the dream, And lighting The Hope.

Song of Martin

I have a dream...
And Martin Luther King

Such a song of soul...
And Martin is a freedom ring

I have a dream...
And all of us, we must sing,
To share the gleams, of his dreams & his song

Vote!

If you do not vote...
You've sought, not to rock the boat

So, if you do...
You help dreams, come through

Thou, you be the guard...
And all, we will stand

With Soul, Heart, and Hand...
To protect our freedoms, so our Land

Voyager

Sky...Wind...Cloud...and Sea
Night...Rain...Stars...and Me

With all these fascination...
And the Rosy imagination

I was alone...
But with my contemplation.

Looking to the far waves...
Coming to the shore and saves

Looking to the brighten star...
Reaching, such a shine spirit, from thee far

Touching the soul of my wander...
Such Rebellious Monk, Into Voyageur anger

Nursing, Tree of own man...
has planted, by the Father of dawn

Thou, upon the code of trust...
The sailing Ship, will sail through, and must,
Must port at its shore, to overcome winds, so the gust.

To Saddam with Love

Saddam...oh Saddam
Good men...never hide
Like a scared child
Do you remembers...
When you invade Kuwait
And Mr. Bush...has kicked your tush,
And now...
When his murder...was in your mind
Mr. Clinton...has kicked your behind
So, again...if you will
Yet, you haven't see the wild bill
Driving you...into fired hell.

Wake up Saddam...You're out of order,
Thou, a little thug...beyond your border
And indeed, you're a dead fox...
Jumped to his own trapbox
What you've done sucks...
And suck...you smell in that corner.

Vote & Deed

Vote; Because if you don't...
    Losing is a right, such a sin you have sought.
Vote; Is the Soul of Liberty...
    So the heart of Freedom, and the Remote.
Vote; Is the Shore of Sea...
    Thou, The Light House to the Voyage Boat.
Vote; Is the Democracy Wind...
    And the Rudder of Direction, So the Float
Vote; Is such the Mind of Liberal...
    Vote, is a Signature on "A Deed," once wrote!

Fission

Too many times while I'm sitting alone...
With lonely thinking, and slow tone
From within, and the thought around me...
Questioning things with nation of what are we
But for somehow that the mind of now...
Become of the ancient searching key
Into universe through wheeling earth...
Between the coil of sun & currents of sea
Crust at depth & sensory chips, has data of reverse...
For both, the Atlantic and the Atlantis debris.

Infants

Through the pattern between Saturn and Mars,
In the moment of Big Bang...
Saturn ran away with the divorced ring
But, the children of death
Were born infants at birth
Between a mother arms, and called earth
All creatures are energy for sails
Voyageurs of males & females...
Thus, their existing of their rebirth!

Words of Truth

To The First Lady, Hillary, And A Sister...
    From One, As A Witness of Society, And A Member

My poem speaks the truth; So the honesty...
    For A great efforts of you; With full integrity

Through A hard work, For classical Health-Care-Reform...
    Taking on Greed; And The Modern-Pharisees, By Storm

Thus, As A Matter Of Fact...
    The Hypocrites are Handcuffed, In Their Act

They lie, And again they will...
    But for sure, The American People, Will give them Hell!

              * * *

Though, about all those Health-Care-Plan...
    Making my comments, As far As I can

One, The Republicans and 'Chafee'...
    Is nothing more than The Rich-Boy-Gravy

Two, The Democrats and 'Cooper'...
    It's no Hit, Thou a little blooper

Three, The President, Which is The One having all...
    Have the right foundation, so the right call

It is touching on all Bases ...
    Thou, scoring home, for all cases

This is The Plan, which has my support...
    Is reasonably, "America First," So with result
        * * *
Though, for Any-Talking-Heads...
    This How The Truth is Stand

And anything else or such, At hand...
    Such, The Ostrich-Heads in The Sand!

The 1992 Presidential Campaign

COMBAT-KID

With my regards, I'm saying hello, SIR,
Thanks, for making me proud of you,
Proud beliefs, America's love we share.

"PEOPLE FIRST" a true massage & everywhere,
"THE CARAVAN" reaching out & Telling you care,
Continued waves, causing BUSH nightmare,
"DON'T STOP" is my wish & It's just fair,
LEONINE campaigning & On the hill be there,
BLINDFOLD OPPOSITION, coming out & you be aware.

"GO AHEAD," with mighty hand of a striking Bear,
"GO AHEAD COMBAT-KID," go ahead with dare,
With no doubt, they will be out,
Out of sight, coming to your net & their own snare

As a running Fox in the middle of a square,
More seeing you, the more he will scare,
Go ahead & march over their despair,
GO AHEAD COMBAT-KID, A FRIEND, AND SIR,
Go ahead, you have mine & EVERYONE'S PRAYER.

"BILL" RINGING BELL

Face To Face...
    You're on A solid Base

You believe in America & yourself...
    So, Also you have the Case

The Case of America's illness...
    With everyday rising, at large pace

The Case of divided Society...
    Since "Reagan," Thou "Bush" the brace.

Face To Face...
    You're on a solid Base

You have the Will, you have the faith...
    You have the skill, and timely race

Face to Face, You're on Solid Base...
    This is a Fact, not just only a phrase

Wandering through the Stars, Into the space...
    Marks A True Leader, Born in Time & Place

Characterized One of The People...
    And for the people, He'll rebuilds, and retrace

"America First" with heart of kindness...
    So great vision, and mind of Ace

Ringing the Bell, seeking "People First"...
    And the people are his home, so his BASE.

Comeback-Kid, Combat-Kid, & Mr. Kid

On November third...
    America will have the call
To write a new history...
    And give the ball
All state will be teammate...
    And you will stand tall.
In my heart, reading the chart, and into my soul...
    Deep down there's a crown & golden stole
The fifty state and more...
    At your door for taking all.
The message of hope, is tomorrow spring...
    With tomorrow's goal.
The message of fear, into the past sear...
    Such leaves in Autumn, alone will fall.
Go ahead Mr. Kid...
    Take our nation, with inspiration to overhaul.
Go ahead stand high & tall...
Go ahead heal America and rebuild
Go ahead start America's future on a roll.
    Go ahead, Comeback-Kid
    Go ahead, Combat-Kid
    Go ahead, Mister-Kid.
These are three characters...
    For masterpiece of control
though, into the history...
    For generation after generation to recall.

Inauguration Song

Tonight's night of joy...
    And time for congratulation
Tonight's in the history's arms
    A birth of nation
This is the era which has just begun...
    To lighting future, with hope & inspiration
Hand and hand, allover our land...
    And from ocean to shiny ocean
We are all in participation...
    At the baby-boomer inauguration.
Voices rising like thunder...
    Singing the song of love...
    thou, the true kinder & gentler.
We're a people of differences; but no separation...
    We are the one-America, the free, and the hope of liberation
We are behind you with all beliefs...
    For tomorrow's proliferation
Though, "people first" is for unity...
    And from generation to generation
Love and harmony under one flag...
    Tonight we begin the celebration.

104 Congress and Majority

The new congress in town...
    Though says, they will legislate
But legislate, was a clown...
    And clowns, govern the home plate
Thus, fair was no verb, nor the noun...
    So indeed was only, a rectorate!
They said "We have a contract...
    And on America, we must act"
But act was a shame...
    And shame is a matter of fact.
The Speaker of the House...
    Here, he comes, and only to change the rule...
    Taking advantage at all of us, so every fool
He talks, offering motion after motion...
    Only, to fit own self, so own illusion.
So with the time go by...
    Chairman after chairman,
    & rep. after rep. stand and imply
But, imply was only for cutting deals...
    And running someone else wheels
Though only "we the people" got the shaft...
    And also we are not in their own draft
So as what it seems...
    They're taking away too many dreams
They've taken away from the poor...
    No mercy   No heart   No cure
They assaulted our constitution...
    And with every turn, with every notion
Though, falsely wants amend "our great
    even for no reason, even with no solution."
They say "unfounded mandate"
    But indeed, is given "federal power"
    And away to "the State!"
They're passing down the buck
    Though, in such a trap,

>   For all us to be stuck!
> Again and here's the 104 Congress and Majority
>   Here comes to the town and seems
>   They're out of governing maturity.
> They said, "Our agenda's a hundred day
>   Though, what all we have,
>   Is only what is the play!!!"
> And though the "play" was far of "truth"
>   And what's good for the "gander"
>   At their mind, is not good for the "goose"!!!

Three Rivers

The secret of the pyramid
For all, so all man

Holding the key of the ancient talisman,
From the pharaohs, so the dawn

Inherited into the house of silence,
For life meaning in plan

Triangle, though, three dimensions,
But, the fourth; is foresee and out of man

Same one; we can see...
Same; zero and based free
Though; the river is one; But three.

North Star

America...and God's country
Dream on...dream with victory
    You're the north star
    Shines in every home
    And reaching very far.

America...The blue skies and free wind
Dream on...Dream tomorrow with no end
    You're the north star
    Shines in every home
    And reaching very far.
America...and mountains high
Dream on...Dream more...Dream and try
    You're the north star
    Shines in every home
    And reaching very far.

Sphinx

The three pyramids of Geza...
Three full dimensions into circle,
Into Sphinx the guard.

Such circle, and cycle of zero,
Such Sphinx & own pharaoh,
Such, Sphinx of beyond.

Such tomorrow, and out of death...
Such tomorrow, and out of birth,
Such tomorrow, and only lives,
Lives foresee; and command!

Cosmos, Age, & Observations

Big bang; began to continue nonstop, for again & yet...
    Into own motion, through energy, directions & every bit.
Though & instead; science, astronomy, & the man of illusion...
    Had observe the universe, with only facts of conclusion.
That only, was the base, based only on what man can see...
    Thus, into wrong knowledge of math, man loosing to foresee.
How can man count the age of space...
    Based only on what seen as the man case.
What's the value of 'zero'...
    If that "one" has lost own base.
Thou, what's the value of 'one'...
    If "zero" & "time," are not being the base.
So; if that in such fact...
    How the numbers will follow,
    Into own logic & own act.
How man can anticipate...
    How the cosmos will reincarnate;
    Without, man, energy, & value in debate.
What's position for the "running-wheel"*...
    With own fuel, energy, & sail.
How much the value, sending to above or reverse...
    Rate of positive, negative, equal, & opposite verse;
    Into three dimensions, time & zero birth.
This & much, same rematch into the silence...
    Into the beyond...so the stage of death.

* Running-wheel: Earth

Witness of Society

I am a witness of era...
    Through a society passing my time
Witnessing the children having sex in early age...
    And the sex only seems their prime
The poetry of their song called rap...
    And rap's wrapped with filth, even if it's rhyme
The sound of the music, so the arts...
    Often conceits the violent, and glorifying the crime
Killing the ills, for somehow they believes!!!
    And somehow their moral of medicine is ethical grime
With sign of governing and politics...
    Signify with mendacity, and low fences for self climb
Thus with media is often built out of hollow...
    Hollow of its own subject, and its core is a core of rime

* * *

The childhood is shorten of its own stage
    And it is no longer become as the age of the child
Drugs, booze, and guns
    In everywhere and nowhere to hide
Broken homes, homeless, and poverty
    Thus, with no adults or a guide
Instead of going to schools to learn
    They learn how to kill or free ride

* * *

Above all, and as God is my witness
That it is not the children's fault
But is a society sown seed of self suicide!

Light Romance

Dance & Romance

What man can say...
Or what the play,
If the both players...
Is only, you & I.

Is it too much...
To know, or such,
We just try...
And ask no why,

I love to dance
I love romance
I love to love you
And take the chance.

What it will be...
If you and me,
Just, for somehow...
We live only for now,
Now and the time...
Singing own Rhyme,
Though, in slaw tone...
We dance alone,
Into the night...
But, not quite,

Till you be in my sight...
And we walks, between candlelight,

Walk and dance
Dream of romance
Dreams into the night.

Paradise

Living time with you...
Seems life in paradise

Paradise only my dreams
To feels what's paradise
Paradise, but it seems
Such castle in the ice
Paradise baby...paradise

If I'm seeking heaven in earth..
Sweetheart, you're the one of my choice

Paradise only my dreams
To feels what's paradise
Paradise, but it seems
Such castle in the ice
Paradise baby...paradise

Holding you love, is my heights...
Breezing you honey & give my life as price

Paradise only my dreams
To feels what's paradise
Paradise, but it seems
Such castle in the ice
Paradise baby...paradise

Such hope...such garden...such your eyes...
Such mist of tomorrow...such morning in blue skies

Paradise only my dreams
To feels what's paradise
Paradise, but it seems
Such castle in the ice
Paradise baby...paradise.

Place in the Heart

In the bottom of my heart,
I kept place for you,
And the key has lost,
Since you baby have gone...
But I was so sure
You will come again
To open your room
And heal my pain.

So many times,
For so many years,
My heart cries out,
And my eyes shading tears & tears...
But I was so sure
You will come again
To open your room
And heal my pain.

Baby...oh my baby,
No cries for yesterday,
or even feels sorrow,
Yesterday was love and memory,
and today hope for tomorrow...
Hope you will come again
To open your room
With love, so no more pain.

Oh Lady

Oh, lady can I have a touch

Oh lady, you mean to me so much,
Oh lady, once we have wish,
For you and I,
We swear to try,
We make love
If ever we have met

Oh lady, you now on my turf,
And I have for you some to give,
It will be for ever, and as far we live,
For you and I,
We swear to try,
We make love,
If we ever have met.

Oh lady, oh my lady,
Let us hold hands, we're ready,

Oh lady, lovely lady,
Tell me if you can,
To kiss you if you wish,
Or let me know, what I do,
If it is too much,
Oh lady, oh lady...
For me and you,
That to be a true,
We will make love,
If we ever have met.

Summer of Love

In hot summer...and blue sea
We in love...you & me

In the hot sun...we in run
You & I...both have fun
Walking on the shore...
Resting under tree...
Living our imagination with souls free

In hot summer...and blue sea
Both we swim...both we flee
Reaching ahead for romance...
And on the middle of island...
You & I holding hand...
You & I...we'll be.

Romance

Do you remember?
      Yes, I do!
What you remember?
      Evcrything, with you!
I remember the birds...
      Singing in the backyard
So your arms around me...
      Holding me strong and hard
Though, odors and scents of you...
      And you and I, not apart
I remember loosen the breath...
      So, taken away my guard!

No More

No more...
I'll come to your door

No more...
And what for

No more...I'll be there...
And why I should care...
For nothing we can share

Can you tell why...
You want me cry
Do you love me...
Or you love the tears in my eye

No more...And it's a shame...
No more...our love be the same

Every word we has said...
Every story we have read
All gone in the flame...
And no more...anyone to blame

In the Wind

In the wind...
We go up and high...

In the wind...
We hope to fly...
We fly high...you & I

In the wind...
We rising wings...
One is you...one is my

In the wind...
We only one...
One we fly...
Live or die...

In the wind, we fly high,
And if we failed...again we try,
In the wind you and I.

A Desire

Boiling water...
And sparkling blue
Flaming fire...
Though, burning my desire

Desire for romance
Desire for one more chance

You touch my heart...
And you wake up my soul
For love at once we have felt
And now seeking my recall

Recalling for romance
Desiring one more chance

Chance to take my imagination
Into my fascination

Fascination in romance
Fascination to enhance.

Why?

I was lonely and walking the shore
Sad I am...
Lonesome I am...
As ever and more

Watched the sun, reaching down for the sea
Such two in love, but not me
I looked above to the sky
Asking why me...why
Why sad I am...
Why...why why?

Heavenly Eyes

For heavenly voice
I have no choice
But to try

Try my best
And never rest
Until you be my

For heavenly eyes
I reach my highs
And through their waves
I want swim
I want fly
Fly high & high
In their blue sky

So we are
Go away & far
And we stay there
Between the star

Want You

When I dance with you...
I want feel your touch
Touching you is my dream...
And dreaming you is a such

When I kiss you...
I want more & much
Much of you always seems...
Is never too much

When I'm with you...
I want have and much
Much of you with me...
Always not much

Love me...
Have me...
I'm yours...
And such.

Such You

Like the rose...you're and much
Full of color & beauty...and such
Such eyes and blue
Such love and true

Like the river...you're and much
Full of life & more...and such
Such eyes and brown
Such deep I'm drown

Like the candle...you're and much
Full of memory & light...and such
Such romance of the nights
So the silence in your heights

Silent Night

At night of silence
And a clock ticking my time
Was shining moon through my glassy window
And I'm waiting for you,
With my rhyme

But the time comes and goes
And I'm holding the red rose
So your favorite wine

After the time gone by
You didn't come
Or tell me hi
I looked to the star
And seems very far
Far and away
As you are

Won't Ask Why?

How I can reach your heart...
Or how I begin or start

I lost my magic, I lost my touch...
So you, have too, and much

What we use to share
No longer become there
All has gone, such nightmare.

More and much...
Less or such
Such time gone by...
And now, you want me cry

No. I'll not cry
No. I'll not try
Nor. Won't ask why?

You Are

If the wind, is only way to fly...
"Sweetheart" you're the wing of my.

If reaching the moon, is only by the eye...
"Honey" you're, only moon of my sky.

If romancing you once, so will die...
Oh "Love," I second the motion, say "I."

If the star, is only rise to its high...
"Baby" you're, the highest of my high.

Bartender

Sunday Night, and sleepy town...
Bartender serving my Beer,
Under candlelight, and Red Gown

She looked to me and said...
I'm a Libra, thou what's your Sign

I looked to her Roman nose...
So her lips, such a living Rose

I said to her, I'm a both crown...
One half Virgo and one half Lion.

She said, you love to touch...
I said, yes and more so much

I was drinking my Beer...
She was sipping her wine

Through, music and slow dance ...
Though, the lips of hers & mine.

Promises

Why don't, you come over tonight...
To share my wine, so my candle light

I swear if you do,
And my dream come through,
I will make it, with you right.

I'll forget the past...
So the silence of the night
I'll forget the time...
And every season of twilight

So if you do,
And my dream come through,
I'll bring the moon for you,
Thou, every star, out of sight.

Please come over tonight...
My heart for you...
Eating me bite by bite.

Life Ordeal

Such a breezy wind, is my dream of you,
Such a gentle rain, and soft morning dew

>This is how I feel
>But my life ordeal
>Won't take my appeal
>Even thou, is due.

Such blue curtain, and golden sea...
Such rising Sun & rays, such you with me

>This is how I feel
>But my life ordeal
>Won't take my appeal
>Even thou, is due.

Such life at best, thou the little once grew,
Such life into nest, and ship of one crew

>This how I feel
>For my life ordeal
>AND EVEN THOUGH...
>I MUST GO!!!
>Though don't matter
>What I feel

Adam and Eve

The love, and the love naive
It's a fact of man happiness,
      also, the man grief

The truth of it,
Is that to give, So to receive

This is the man story,
Since Adam, takes the Apple, from Eve

Even thou, out of the simple belief...
Who's the sinner, is Adam or Eve!!!

It's at both end, with each own believe...
Adam want the Apple, and the Apples belong to Eve!

* To the tune of *Adam's Apple*.

How Could I?

How could I...When I go by
I won't smile...Or say hi

How can I hide...When you're around
Won't be in mind.. I want you in my side
Thou, I wish to say hello...
 And You & I, Go for the ride

Go away and free
Just you & me
Hand 'n' hand, so side by side

Lifetime

Love and lifetime. Both...
    Such a Train for Two

On one road, and distend destiny ...
    So, the passing stations, are passing through

Although, the time comes to the ages ...
    Into different stages,
    Thou, the stages, comes & goes.

Love Song

For you Erica Lee...
    I'll ride the HI waves, and the deep Sea

I'll walk the Moon, and search every Star...
    Thou, marching on the valley, through the hills, and far

I'll asks the Birds, and every moving thing...
    About you Erica, So my Ring

So, if the ring is mine...
    Erica's meant to be,
    Such a song, at once I had sing.

Up Side-Down!

Why, my life have been up side-down,
Does the reason is, changing my drinks,
From Egyptian "OUZO," to Missourian "WINE!"

So, why the guilt, has been felt,
Even thou, is not my own.
Does the reason, won't be in the same season,
And our music, won't play on the same tone!

Seeking the reasons, or the cause,
The only answer, is just because,
Sometimes things are, How are things goes!

Why, between her and me,
Both, we never can agree,
Even on the color of "a green tree!"

Thou, if the complacency, was self deceit,
Then, the different, was such "HEAD" & "FEET!"

Philosophy & Thoughts

The Three Elements

UNIFICATION

The art of words, not only rhyming verse...
Is the art of thought, and its reverse

The reality of man is three elements...
The fact of life, is begins at birth

One, we have come,
Two, we are here,
Three, we will go.

Thus, the modification of one & three...
It is the modifier, so the fact's two

Wisdom's believing life, not only passing through...
But is a bridge, for everyone to undergo

Those are three unifying elements of plateau...
Universal of inspiration, live and die under nature law.

Evolution, Revolution Into Re-

Thinking of the notion...Who are we?
Through the motion...And sounding free

That One, we were the Evolution...
And the Two, We are the Revolution,
So the Three is the coming, Will be

Will be such stage of Third angel...
Such the Pre-. To the Re-.

Such a Triangle, through a cycle...
Thou every cycle, into Circle, began of Zero Degree.

Universe, Sea, and Stone

Why the modern man goes to the moon,,
And why curing the ruined;
With adding, more and more ruin.

Isn't indeed, man's greed,
Is road to defied, and for self own.

Are we the twin, of the original sin,
And to self distraction, we're in tune.

Isn't the mystery, of our ancient history,
Is the phenomena, of the unknown.

Does the Pyramid, in the four dimensions,
Such the nature, on its four faces, in tone,
Through, Three visible elements, and what's belong,
The majestic universe, deep secrecy in sea, and power of stone!

Fate

What the fate is having for me...
    And what of tomorrow, is will be!
Though, and above all...
    I will seek to rise, even into the fall
So learning out of all to conjure up wise...
    And picking up my rubbles, but not demise
Believing gives, takes, and ties...
    Into destiny, into life, so the compromise
So we all the same; with only difference...
    Between the good, and the otherwise!

Life & Thoughts

Thinking of Life!
    And through the term of "Desire,"
Though, into thinking of the Gold...
    And its purity, always comes out of Fire!

Thinking to reason of the "Why"...
    And why that is the require?
With self answer, and into form of art...
    In such candle, one part is fire, so a light.

Thinking of life...
    In such time of the "Far,"
Into forward is free...
    And backward is into the bar!

Wise Man

These are the words my father has said:
As it is great to follow the inter sense,

As well is greater, knowing how to hold.

Mind never be at absent,
Mind knowing now from tomorrow,
Though, looking then, so the unfold.

Such Man's!

Thinking of Man's life, After birth...
    Into the motions of fact, unto death
    Though, same god, some bad, and some such myth.
    Such Zoo...Such Jangles, Such Sea & Earth...
    Such Strong & Weak, Such rising to above,
    Or falling into the darkness of depth.

Thinking of Man; Meaning of hope & steps...
    Such kismet into reaching destiny,
    Or such, some doomed, to hold the fallen grips.
    Such the Angels of Us, and the Guardians of bless...
    Or such the Weirdos; And the Weird, be reverse!

Logic

As, romance inspires out of candles...
As well, the Candle burning itself

Though, both in the eye of fairness...
Are fair, in both term and turf.

As, positive time positive...
Is equal positive, and true
As well, negative time negative...
Is equal positive, in reverse too.

Man and Free

I hope I'm not only one, is left to sing
Thou, if I am alone,
Alone, will enter to the ring.

Perhaps, I will take some hits,
Or perhaps, alone I will stand,
But, I will fight with every bits,
Even, if I only have one hand.

I will build every bridge,
And I will reach every grand
The truth is the fire of my pledge,
As well that love & peace is my brand.

I will cross every river,
I will swim every sea,
And never to say never...
Because am man, and I'm free

Life

Man's life is man's gift,
Such a time through circle,
Thus...a rising sun,
And the sun rise, for never set.

Reasoning

As in the heart of nights and always,
For the day that's the begin

As well, the sin of sin is not the exit,
But it is the "in"

Also, there's no lost wisdom,
To override own justice,
If based on now, with modifying then

Thou, as tomorrow is a true value,
As well, the now and based on then

Such the math is based on zero,
And zero is equal none

But also, that the same zero,
Constituted the one and facts the ten.

Birthday

A birthday...
To everyone it is the same,
But also, it's a different,
From any other day.

A birthday...
None of us can remembers,
Even though, we grew up and learns,
Learned to get older and celebrate!

Man!

Bread & Blood...
Into the meaning of man,
So the God.

Bread & Blood...
They're the Christians moral believe,
Example of communion & a bond.

Such air, water, fire, and land...
Four dimensions
But, three at hand.

So the nature, so we...
Four at dimensions, but lawful three,
Law of nature, law of man, and stand.

* To the tune of *Christ Sacrifice*.

Dust & Earth

We the children of the nature...
    And form both genders we got born

Sperm and egg, the base of fetus...
    So fetus itself, is process minus, such seeding corn.

At time of zero, from the soul-mother, at birth...
    Though, into life and the fact of numbers,
    So into time, and nature-mother, modifying death.

This is the one story, though the man wealth...
    Through elements of reality, and elements of myth,
    Part of it is Dust, and part of it is Earth.

Wine & Wheat

Wine & wheat...wheat & wine
Is the blood & into fiber
Though, is the fiber...into soul divine.

It is the weeding party...
And Christ was the guest
Creating the wine, is a way to define...
That Christ example, is joining the rest.

It is the thanks, so the gives...
It is Christ, and how he lives
Giving the bread...and Christ was sent
For the common cause...under one dome & a tent!!!

Power of Thee Word

The power of thee the word!!!
    It is the Christianity moral beliefs
    So it's divine & the father of the Lord.

The power of thee word!!!
    It is the philosophy of art, into thoughts,
    Though, the Bible of Holiness, is a written word.

The power of thee word!!!
    It is the life of Moses, so the Christ,
    And though the disciples, into the same "line of gold!"

The power of thee word!!!
    It is the poetry of King David, so the "wise"
    And everyone after, for to honor & behold!

* * *

The power of thee word!!!
    It can move mountains & destroy castles,
    And it can live, die, bought, and sold!

The power of thee word!!!
    It is the God of "love" & God of "hate"
    Thus, into the silence of the "pharaoh"
    On such "stone" as is written & told!

The power of thee word!!!
    It is the history & it's the DEED,
    Though, it lives into thee "FOLD" & THEE "UNFOLD!!!"

Words of Wisdom

These are the words...
The wise man has said, so my dad

That's happier to think happy...
Even if you are sad!

The sophistication of 'simple' is its wisdom...
But the same and wiser, for known what's odd!

As the logic of numbers...
Constitute 'minus' to fact 'even'

As well the same that logic of math...
Applies own wisdom to be remembers
That the basic & value of original, has begun with 'add'!

Baseball

Outfield angels & watchers for the hill...
Left and right-right handed controls the mound,
sailing the game into happy mill.

It is a magic of three bases...
But, four defensive to alter & dwell.

So, for reaching the home plate...
Is everyone in the team work, so the fate.
Though, it is not easy, nor for to kill...
Into catcher, guarding the home, with fiery hell.

So when listening to the fans say hey & hey...
It's the beer working & the home team in play.

Hey more & more, in such voices roars and roar...
A single, double, triple, and home run sure score.

We hope grand slam...
Even if it's full of cheese 'n' ham.
A gift of Uncle Sam!

Umpire digging down...
Calling balls and strikes in sound of hewn.
Even with angry fan shouting and clown...
To bring the bench hitter to put the game down.

Now, is the seventh inning stretch
& fans running to the restrooms
Seems they have a train they must catch.

The ninth inning & standing ball park...
Want it over before dark.
It is the baseball & and game in such stark...
In such fashion of the ancient, so the Noachian Ark.

Baseball's America's pastime with no doubt...
It has the numbers, four balls in & three strikes out.
It is a game of fascination...
Triangle powers, into a pyramid of participation!!!

Children & Religion

The Joys of the Seasons

The birth and time for renew
Soft such love for you & you
Peace such flakes of snow
Gently flow and flow

Flakes covering the valley...
And the green
Covering the mountain...
Such a white crown...
On the heads queen

The birth and time for renew
Soft such love for you & you
Peace such flakes of snow
Gently flow and flow

From the time of thanksgiving...
Into the time of goodwill
The sound of angels singing...
Merry Christmas and joyeux noel

The birth and time for renew
Soft such love for you & you
Peace such flakes of snow
Gently flow and flow

Time of Christmas is time of hope...
And hope is tomorrow and tomorrow new year
Though ahead is the Spring...is near

The birth and time for renew
Soft such love for you & you
Peace such flakes of snow
Gently flow and flow

* To the tune of *Christmas*.

One Two Three

One two three
We all born, we all free.

Two three four,
We learn more and more.
One two three,
Sun, river, and tree,
the sun lives in the sky,
For shining the morning, for you and I
So the river lives in land,
For the water we drink, and clean our hand.

One two three,
Moon, stars and sea,
God made those, for you and me.

One two three,
We all are born, and we all free.

Learning

One...Two
Me...and You.

Three...four...five
Sister & Brother
Father & Mother
Husband & Wife.

Six...Seven...Eight
House & Tree
River & Sea
Rain & Cate.

Nine...Ten
Girls & Boys
Women & Men

Thou, for after & before...
We grow up & learn more & more.

* Children's tune.

The High-Rank

For the God's my thank...
    Believing the Lord, is my High-Rank

He lives above in the sky...
    Watching for you and I

He's around us and through...
    For protecting me and you

He lives everywhere and free...
    In the River, in the farm, in the tree

He lives every were, want to be...
    In the mountain, in the town, in the sea.

The Kids

GROWING UP

I love Mama...
I love Papa, family, and friend.

I wash my hands...
I clean my teeth, because I'm a good kid.

I know to pray...
I sleep early...
And in the morning I fix my bed.

I'm no fool...
Because I go the school

I learn the math & sciences...
So the arts and every tool.

Prayers & Wonders

When I wake in the morning...
I cross my face, so my heart, and pray

Pray for The Lord, and say...
Gives us happiness, and take sadness away

               * * *

With truth of mind...
Just looking around...
Everything we'll find...
Have a sense of God say.

               * * *

Wandering around, simple to know...
Closer to God, close we go

Wandering around, with faith & true...
Much will sound, even the silent, move through

Through every voice, every word will say...
Far we go, far we choose to obey.

* Children's tune.

Mary & Son

To us God has sent his Own Son,
For teaching and seeking result,
Though Heaven is glory,
And Hell is not The Christ fault.

Oh, Messiah, Oh, Emanuel,
Oh, Mary & Mother of renewal

Oh, Queen of Queens,
A burning bush, thou virgin of mean

You are the crown of kindness,
Though Your son is the king of bless.

Overcome the Death "The Christ"

Indeed He rose, and overcame the Death...
    The King of Peace, and Prince of Earth

The Father forces, moved the heavy Stone...
    To left the Son to his Right, so the Throne

The Roman Guards, became blinds from his light...
    But the Disciples, so the believers,
    Saw him again, and by Eyes, so insight
    Alleluia...alleluia, the Christ rose, with no doubt
    Alleluia...alleluia, the Christ rose...
    And his rising lives in our hearts.

Again We'll Meet

From my chimney...
      And under my roof,
Santa comes and says Ho Ho Ho...
      Though, I have proof.

We have the Christmas...
      & we have the tree,
We have the Christmas lights...
      For the child Christ was born & free.

      We've gifts...Wise men 'says'
      So Joseph, Mary and New "Days"

How is wonderful...How is sweet
Christ's Birth True...& again we'll meet.

The Four Seasons

Winter

While Autumn leaving the land...
    Through Nature order, and the Nature hand
Cold and touching river and tree...
    Mountain, farm, and sea.

Winter such time, so the unfold...
    Some of it young, some of it old,
    So, some others at certain, thou at hold.

Winter, and for somehow...
    Bring lovers together, to hold & vow!

Somehow we knows the warmth out of cold...
    And somehow the story of man,
    Such chapter, has been written, and told!

Spring

When the long nights become shorter,
And the motion of the Ocean,
Melting the snow, and the icy winter.

So, the Spring tells the cold, time to go...
Time for opening the buds,
And time, for the young to grow.

Spring, is the nature arts, of its own,
But others, such copy, or original, and drawn.

Spring is the beauty of virgin breeze...
Sweet odder, fully colors, fresh & ease.

Summer

The summer is marching...
Thou, the sun his backbones

Sending the warmness into Earth & Sea...
Through the creatures and life tones

Thus, for lovers is a life concepts...
The glory for success, and fixing for the rowen

Some, such opening rose at Spring...
And some, such fallen leaves at Autumn's falling alone!

Autumn

Why the Autumn, takes away the leaves, from the Tree,
And why the Nature, for this matter, seemly agree!

Does the beauty of the nudity...
Forced the Fall to kneel in his own Knee
Or is the joy of love and making...
Create the comfort into the purity of high degree

Also, for the true sense of romance...
With conative warmth, even of the apogee

Believing, for somehow, that Nature & Man...
Matching the same, since the time of dawn,
Thou, born and live, so will die and free.

Afterward

The last verse in the poem "Four Seasons":

"Believing, for somehow, that Nature and Man...
Matching the same, since the time of dawn,
Thou, born and live, so will die & free."

The above verse was inspired by the Bible verse "Ash for ash, Dust for Dust." To me that means: We come from Nature. We live in Nature. We will die by the laws of Nature. This is also how Christ was created and how man was made.

Nevertheless, the laws of man were created to govern civility and to organize capitalistic systems. This in itself means to remove man from **Jungle Rule**, which is governed by Nature. We often use the phrase "Jungle Rule" to describe vicious acts.

By now you might be wondering what my beliefs about **romance** are, particularly because this is the central word of my book. I cannot find a word that more accurately describes romance than **harmony**, which in itself means the love of nature. Because we are a part of nature and romance itself is governed by nature, what act of man is more governed by nature than the **sexual desire**. We must remember that sexual desires are governed under the wing of romance and are shaped through home life and academic life. As **civility** is the law of man and the **Jungle Rules** are governed by nature, romance is with both the rule of civility and the rule of the jungle.

Because the above thought is in line with the "nature & man" according to the law of romance, I also believe in the Bible's definition of romance as a mirage and a vow. I paraphrased this belief in "Twin But One," which approached the united act of making love as a step into the spiritual order and romance. Here we shall ask ourselves in what motion is the human being **assembled**—not as **two**, but as **one** by the act of love making. This is the face of **romance**, as opposed to the face of **bondage**. It is greatly influenced by what we learned and experienced in our childhood fantasies. Thus, INPUT=OUTPUT, or close to it!

Thinking in the above manner as to why a man loves a woman, for me it is based on three reasons—plus one more which is composed of my Mother as One, my Sister as One, and I have or will make love to One. This leads to the power of the Fourth Dimension which is the "Twin But One." This is the same for both genders. Mathematically it means that two halves=one.

Well now my readers, before I close this final page, I would like to let you know that for me all of my poems are like my children, and in a way some of them might make you laugh or cry. Perhaps they will even ignite the imagination, but above all I have always hoped that as children they have behaved with good manners. I also hope that we will be invited to enjoy your company and pleasure again.

In closing I leave you in God speed, and also with this thought.

>	Won't say good-bye...
>	Would say so long
>	For good-bye feels alone...
>	But the hope's tomorrow's song.
>	So, see you again is my hope...
>	Health and happiness & so strong.

Truly,
Chris A. Misdary
The Author